T0419293

MOON LANDINGS

BY DALTON RAINS

Apex is distributed by North Star Editions:
sales@northstareditions.com | 888-417-0195

Produced for Apex by Red Line Editorial.

Photographs ©: NASA, cover, 1, 4–5, 6, 8, 13, 14, 15, 16–17, 18–19, 20–21; AP Images, 7, 12; iStockphoto, 10–11; Goddard/NASA, 22–23, 29; Brandon Hancock/NASA, 24; Eric Bordelon/NASA, 26–27

Library of Congress Control Number: 2023910088

ISBN
978-1-63738-738-2 (hardcover)
978-1-63738-781-8 (paperback)
978-1-63738-866-2 (ebook pdf)
978-1-63738-824-2 (hosted ebook)

Printed in the United States of America
Mankato, MN
012024

NOTE TO PARENTS AND EDUCATORS

Apex books are designed to build literacy skills in striving readers. Exciting, high-interest content attracts and holds readers' attention. The text is carefully leveled to allow students to achieve success quickly. Additional features, such as bolded glossary words for difficult terms, help build comprehension.

TABLE OF CONTENTS

CHAPTER 1

APOLLO 11

A spacecraft nears the surface of the Moon. Two **astronauts** sit inside the **lunar lander**. Neil Armstrong is the commander. He finds a flat spot to land.

The spacecraft that reached the Moon was a lunar lander called the Apollo Lunar Module.

The spacecraft lands.
Armstrong climbs down a ladder.
He steps onto the surface. He is
the first person on the Moon.

Neil Armstrong was an astronaut from 1962 to 1971.

The first Moon landing was one of the most-viewed events of all time. About 650 million people watched it.

FAST FACT

After stepping on the Moon, Armstrong said, "That's one small step for man, one giant leap for mankind."

A second astronaut joins Armstrong. They explore for more than two hours. They collect **samples** and take photos. Then the two astronauts return to the spacecraft. They prepare to fly back to Earth.

THREE-PART SPACECRAFT

The Apollo 11 spacecraft had three sections. One part went down to the Moon's surface. In another part, an astronaut stayed in **orbit**. The third part held fuel. It held a rocket engine, too.

 Buzz Aldrin was the second person on the Moon.

CHAPTER 2

EARLY MOON MISSIONS

Countries began trying to explore the Moon in the 1950s. The **Soviet Union** and United States were two of the main countries. First, they sent robots and spacecraft without people.

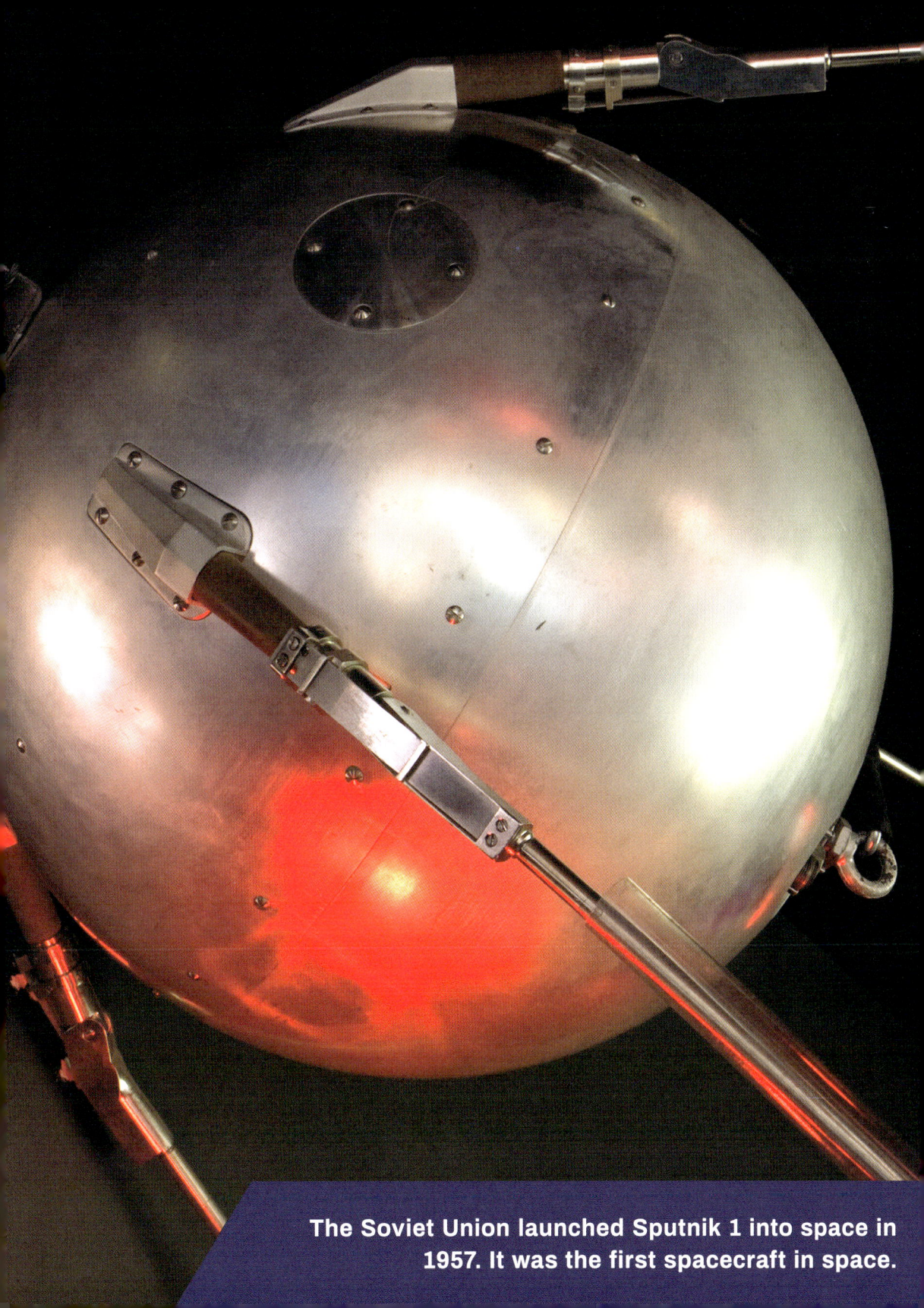

The Soviet Union launched Sputnik 1 into space in 1957. It was the first spacecraft in space.

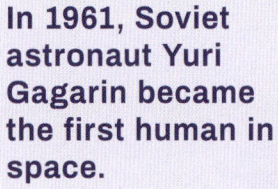

In 1961, Soviet astronaut Yuri Gagarin became the first human in space.

They wanted to send people next. **NASA** started trying in 1961. It began the Apollo program. In 1968, astronauts orbited the Moon during Apollo 8.

The Apollo 8 mission took photos of Earth from near the Moon's surface.

THE SPACE RACE

The United States and the Soviet Union both wanted to get to the Moon first. They made new machines and tools. The **competition** was called the Space Race.

When Apollo astronauts returned to Earth, they landed in the ocean.

Apollo 10 launched in 1969. Three astronauts orbited the Moon. Two got into a lunar lander. They flew closer to the surface. But they did not land.

A Saturn V rocket gets ready to launch for the Apollo 10 mission.

CHAPTER 3

MOON LANDINGS

The Apollo 11 mission finally sent astronauts to the Moon's surface. The trip to the Moon took more than three days.

The astronauts put an American flag on the Moon during the Apollo 11 mission.

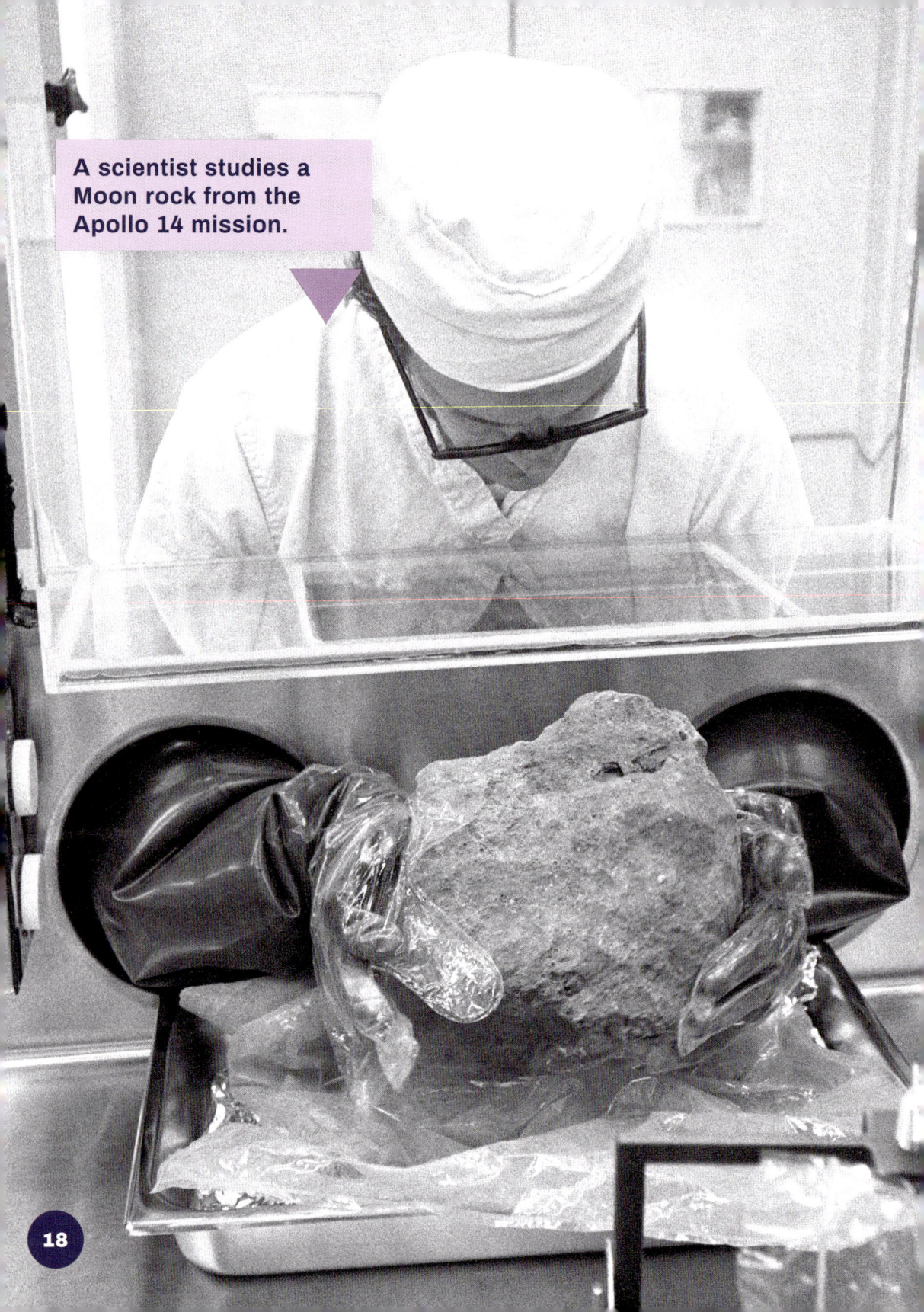

A scientist studies a Moon rock from the Apollo 14 mission.

More people went to the Moon with Apollo 12 and Apollo 14. They brought rocks and soil samples back to Earth. That helped scientists learn about the history of the Moon.

APOLLO 13

Apollo 13 didn't go as planned. The astronauts were going to the Moon. But there was a problem with their spacecraft. They had to return to Earth early.

The Lunar Roving Vehicle could drive up to 12 miles per hour (19 km/h).

The last three Apollo missions lasted longer. Astronauts stayed on the Moon for three days at a time.

FAST FACT

NASA sent a Lunar Roving Vehicle to the Moon for later Apollo missions. It let astronauts drive around.

CHAPTER 4

AFTER APOLLO

After Apollo 17, Moon landings stopped. That was in 1972. But the United States still sent spacecraft to study it. Other countries did, too.

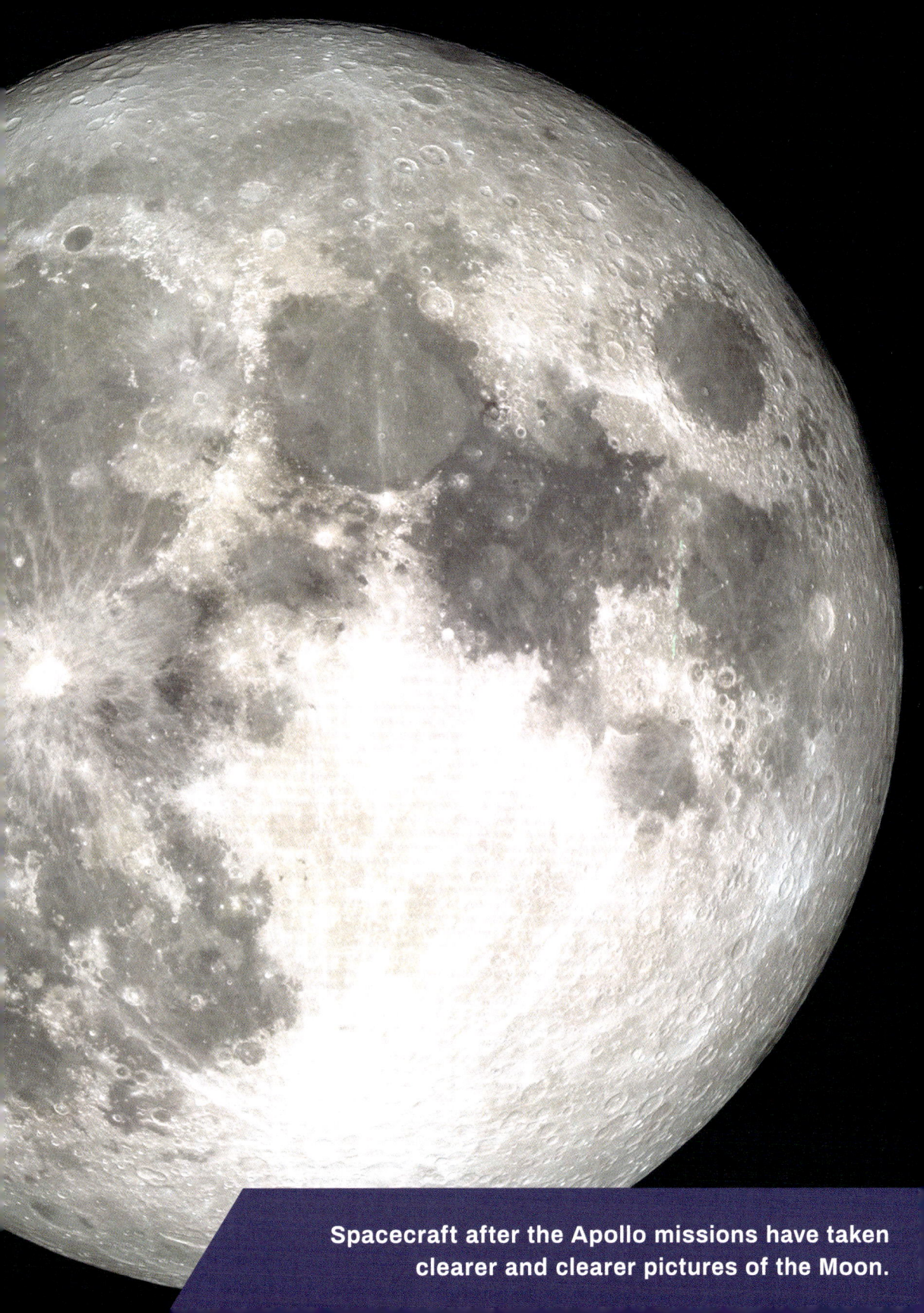

Spacecraft after the Apollo missions have taken clearer and clearer pictures of the Moon.

24

No Moon landings happened for many years. But NASA took a first step in 2022. The Artemis I mission launched. It tested the new Orion spacecraft.

FAST FACT

The Orion spacecraft can hold up to four astronauts.

◀ **Artemis I does a test launch in November 2022.**

In February 2023, NASA put together parts of the rocket for Artemis II.

FWD A

Next, NASA planned to send astronauts around the Moon. The mission would be called Artemis II. It would prepare for a third mission. NASA hoped to land people on the Moon again.

BASE CAMP

NASA planned to assemble a new **space station**. It would orbit the Moon. NASA also planned to make a base camp for future Moon missions.

COMPREHENSION QUESTIONS

Write your answers on a separate piece of paper.

1. Write a few sentences that explain the main ideas of Chapter 3.

2. Which Moon mission do you find most interesting? Why?

3. In which mission did astronauts first orbit the Moon?

    A. Apollo 8

    B. Apollo 11

    C. Apollo 13

4. Why have astronauts not stayed on the Moon for more than a few days?

    A. Astronauts take years to reach the Moon.

    B. It is hard for people to survive on the Moon.

    C. People already fully understand the Moon.

5. What does **sections** mean in this book?

*The Apollo 11 spacecraft had three **sections**. One part went down to the Moon's surface. In another part, an astronaut stayed in orbit.*

   A. kinds of rockets

   B. different pieces or parts

   C. doors to the outside

6. What does **assemble** mean in this book?

*NASA planned to **assemble** a new space station. It would orbit the Moon.*

   A. build

   B. destroy

   C. move away

Answer key on page 32.

GLOSSARY

astronauts
People who are trained to travel in a spacecraft.

competition
An event where people or groups try to beat others.

lunar lander
The part of a spacecraft that lands on the Moon.

NASA
Short for National Aeronautics and Space Administration.
NASA is the United States' space organization.

orbit
A curved path around an object in space.

samples
Small amounts of a material that scientists collect and study.

Soviet Union
A country in Europe and Asia that existed from 1922 to 1991.

space station
A spacecraft where astronauts can live. It orbits a planet or
a moon.

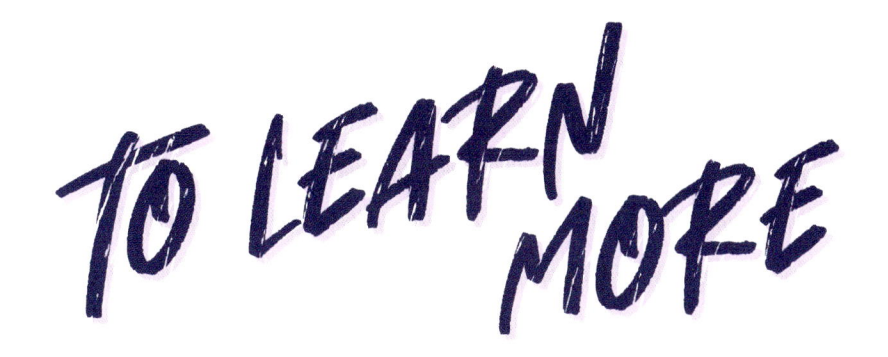

BOOKS

Huddleston, Emma. *Explore the Moon*. Minneapolis: Abdo Publishing, 2022.

Mattern, Joanne. *The Moon*. Mendota Heights, MN: Focus Readers, 2023.

Sommer, Nathan. *The Moon*. Minneapolis: Bellwether Media, 2019.

ONLINE RESOURCES

Visit **www.apexeditions.com** to find links and resources related to this title.

ABOUT THE AUTHOR

Dalton Rains is an author and editor from Saint Paul, Minnesota. He loves to learn about new science discoveries.

INDEX

ANSWER KEY:
1. Answers will vary; 2. Answers will vary; 3. A; 4. B; 5. B; 6. A